CW01429033

We are a creative meritocracy where the best ideas are promoted. ━━━━
Individually and collectively we are developing propositions that contribute to a broader architectural debate, which encompasses aesthetics, environment, politics, economics and ethics. Every project makes a value statement: about those who created it, those who commissioned it, and the cultural and physical contexts within which it was created. The projects illustrated in this book give an insight into these values and preoccupations. Projects such as London Business School (page 10) won in competition this year investigate the notion of education as business. Scissors (page 6), a new building for a major Italian fashion design house, looks at a series of complex issues, from the idea of building as brand catalyst to modernity in the context of a Grade I listed building. SixtyK house (page 14) challenges preconceptions of affordability and volume house-building. Our carpark at Penrith (page 20) is an exercise in site-specific form generation and The Alan Turing Building (page 40) at the University of Manchester features the largest photovoltaic array in the north-west of England. The shortlisted competition entry for the Strabane bridges (page 50) in Northern Ireland takes its cue from the town's existing historic bridge and creates something original without resorting to predictable structural gymnastics. The fit-out for the London Development Agency (page 56) by ID:SR amplifies the qualities of the agency and its branding, creating a seamless journey from the streetscape to the workplace. 399 Edgware (page 72) is a project much praised by CABE as an example of how to deal with high density, city fringe, mixed-use retail and residential buildings, and Monument (page 88) takes as its starting point an historic position in the City of London, engaging with this history to create a memorable and responsive form. Lowther Castle and Gardens (page 94) works at several levels to create a cultural complex of international significance. Designed around a 19th century ruined castle and forgotten gardens, this project is truly unique. Ashford Learning Campus (page 104) uses concepts of fluidity and movement to generate plan and form. The Mathematics Building for the University of Bristol (page 110) has been developed in close conjunction with the mathematicians whose desire for visible idea creation and interaction has had a significant influence over the architecture. The first residents moved into Carabanchel 19 (page 116) in March 2007. This is the latest public housing development for the Madrid housing authority, EMVS, whose ambition is to dignify and innovate the programme of housing across Spain, and Lighthouse (page 142) is a high performance prototype sustainable home for the Building Research Establishment – the first net zero carbon house in the UK. ━━━━ We seek out projects which enable us to actively engage in a process which involves unbridled imagination and rigorous critique. We don't have a formulaic response, but search for the differentiator, the special, the extraordinary in each of these projects. We embrace our diversity and we will work with anybody who excites and interests us. We are motivated by many things and gauge our own success in many ways. ━━━━ This book is intended as a rough guide to our combined creative output over the past 12 months. ━━━━ We hope you enjoy it. ━━━━ SR May 2007 ━━━━

Selected work 2006–2007

University of Bristol — 110
ITV — 112
Dalston — 114
Carabanchel 19 — 116

02.2007

Bessemer Building — 122
Aeronautics Faculty — 124
40 Fountain Street — 126

03.2007

InQbate — 130
Northern General Hospital — 134

04.2007

Primrose Hill — 138
Crawley New Town Hall — 140
Lighthouse — 142
Funlab — 144

05.2007

Penrith Carpark — 020
Red Bull — 024

06.2006

City Quarter — 028
Salvation Army headquarters — 032

07.2006

The Alan Turing Building — 040
New Bodleian Library — 042

08.2006

Gambling Commission — 046
Arup headquarters phases 2 and 3 — 048
Strabane Bridges — 050

09.2006

05.2006

004

Projects in May —— Scissors —— London Business School —— SixtyK

Two parallelograms, one inverted and superimposed on the other, generate a heroic 26 metre cantilever. This acts as a navigational device enabling a series of views through to the Grade I listed John Rylands University Library and the shifting pedestrian route from the Town Hall civic core to the heart of Spinningfields. Diagonally expressed, solid, translucent and transparent panels track the three storey upper level truss, respond to the leaded window tracery of the Neo-Gothic library and emulate the weave of cloth, linking back to the textile history of the area. ▬▬▬

Project: Scissors ▬▬▬ Location: The Avenue, Spinningfields, Manchester

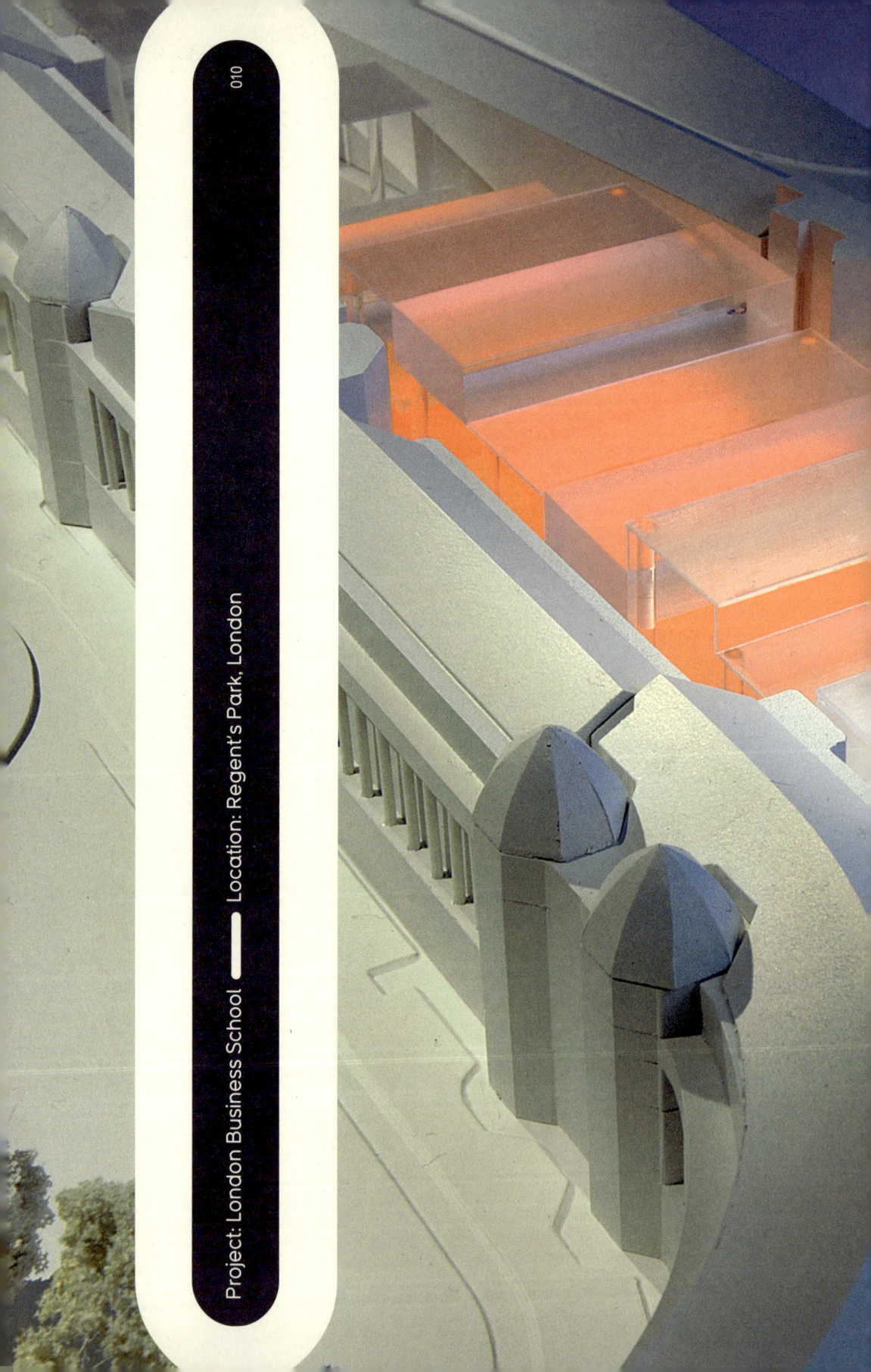

Project: London Business School — Location: Regent's Park, London

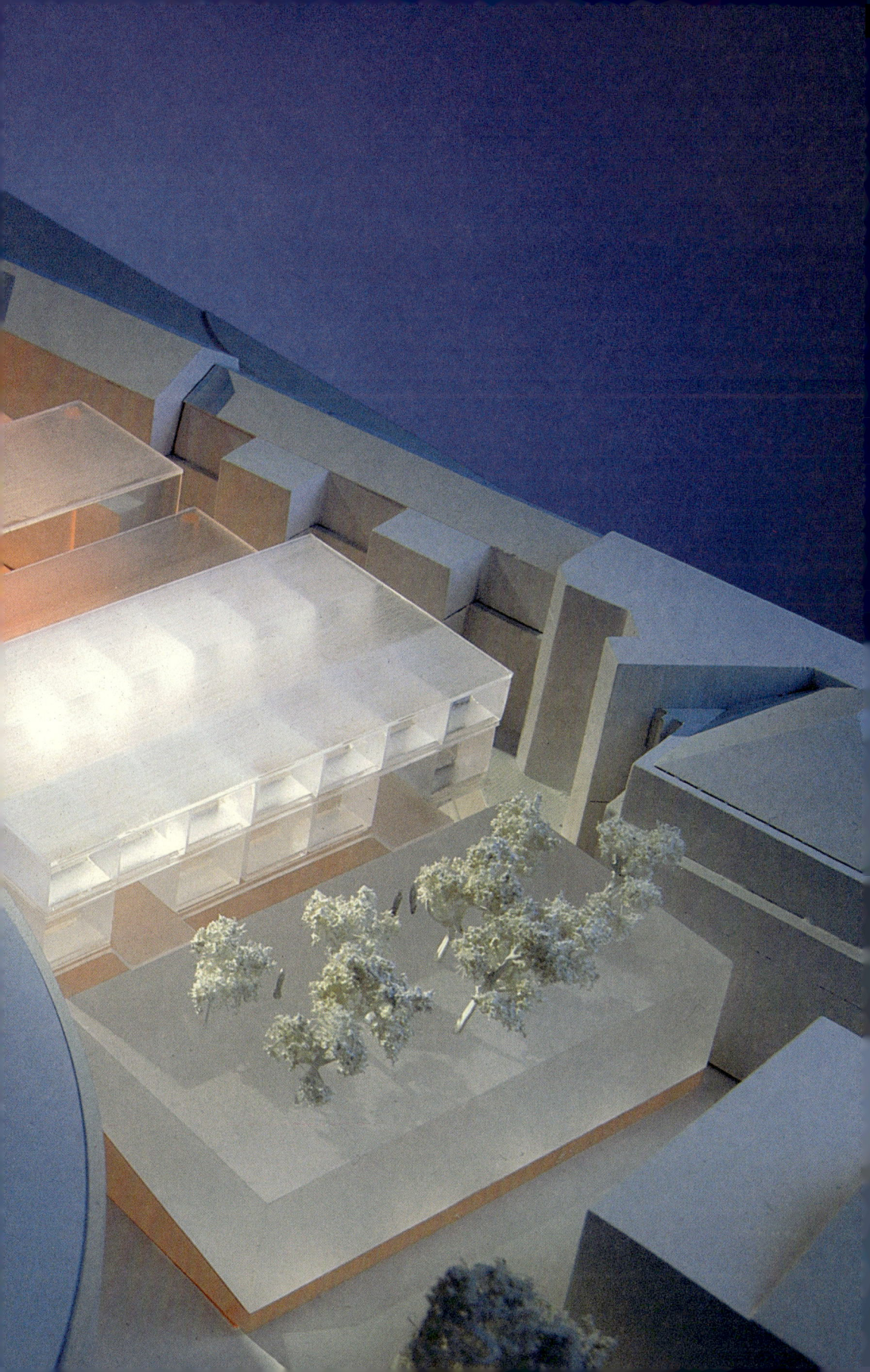

A procession of spaces creates this 'amphitheatre of business'. Three inhabited 'bridges', avoiding the predictable gridshell, create a sense of drama and intimacy and span the gap between London Business School's Nash terrace facing Regent's Park and another facing Park Road. Expressed in glass and steel, they oversail the central forum, creating a dramatic, staggered roofline and infuse the internal spaces with a variety of light conditions by day and night. ▬

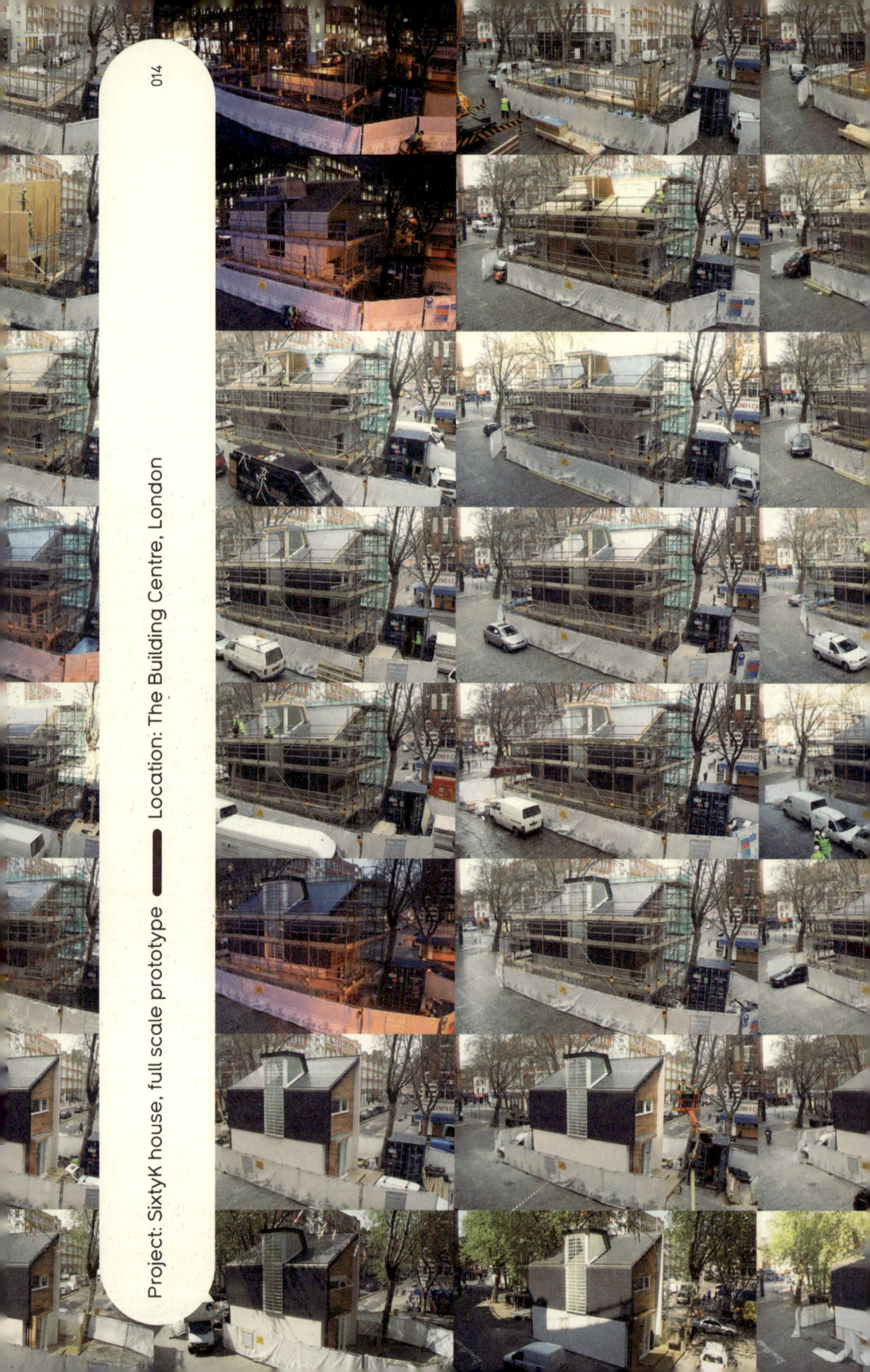

Project: SixtyK house, full scale prototype —— Location: The Building Centre, London

There is space to swing
both a cat and its kittens
and not a mock-Tudor
window in sight.

The Guardian, 13 May 2006

06.20.06

Projects in June —— Penrith Carpark —— Red Bull

SHAW 22

The beauty and extreme variety in the landscape of the Lake District was something we very much wanted to embody and capture as accurately as possible. To do this we created a digital representation of the topography of the area and extracted a slice to create a template for the facade. Each of the 1,622 timber strips are uniquely cut and pre-assembled to provide a constantly evolving form of varying shadow patterns. ▬

Location: Penrith, Cumbria

Project: Carpark

The practice's founder
must be turning in his grave.

Letter to the Cumberland and
West Moreland Herald, 10 June 2006

Project: Red Bull ———— Location: London

The form and elements of the concept are derived from the iconic Red Bull can.

07.20.06

Projects in July — City Quarter — Salvation Army headquarters

028

City Quarter is a deal
more thoughtful than
some. It is relatively
understated, intelligently
laid out, promises to be
built of good durable
materials and will
start to bring some
sense to what has been
for years a largely
forgotten backland.

Hugh Pearman, The Sunday Times,
10 June 2006

Project: City Quarter ⎯ Location: Aldgate, London

The brief was simple...modern in design, frugal in operation, evangelical in purpose.

Jesus said, "I have come into the world as

08.2006

Projects in August —— The Alan Turing Building —— New Bodleian Library

bute bute bute bute bute

camira

DESIGN TEX

the Zodiac

Three sliding ingots, defined by a fully glazed atrium, create academic transparency and physical permeability for the mathematics, physics and photon science departments (AMPPS). The building sits between the newly create University Place on the northern frontier of the campus, the cantilevered projects 'pushing' and 'pulling' across the urban surrounding. An oversailing roof houses the largest photovoltaic array in the north-west of England, with potential savings of over 17,000kgs of carbon dioxide per annum. ━━

Project: New Bodleian Library ⟶ Location: University of Oxford

A monolithic vault for the University's special book
collections, lurking at the core of the existing library.

NEW BODLEIAN LIBRARY

09.2006

Projects in September ▬ Gambling Commission ▬ Arup headquarters ▬ Strabane Bridges

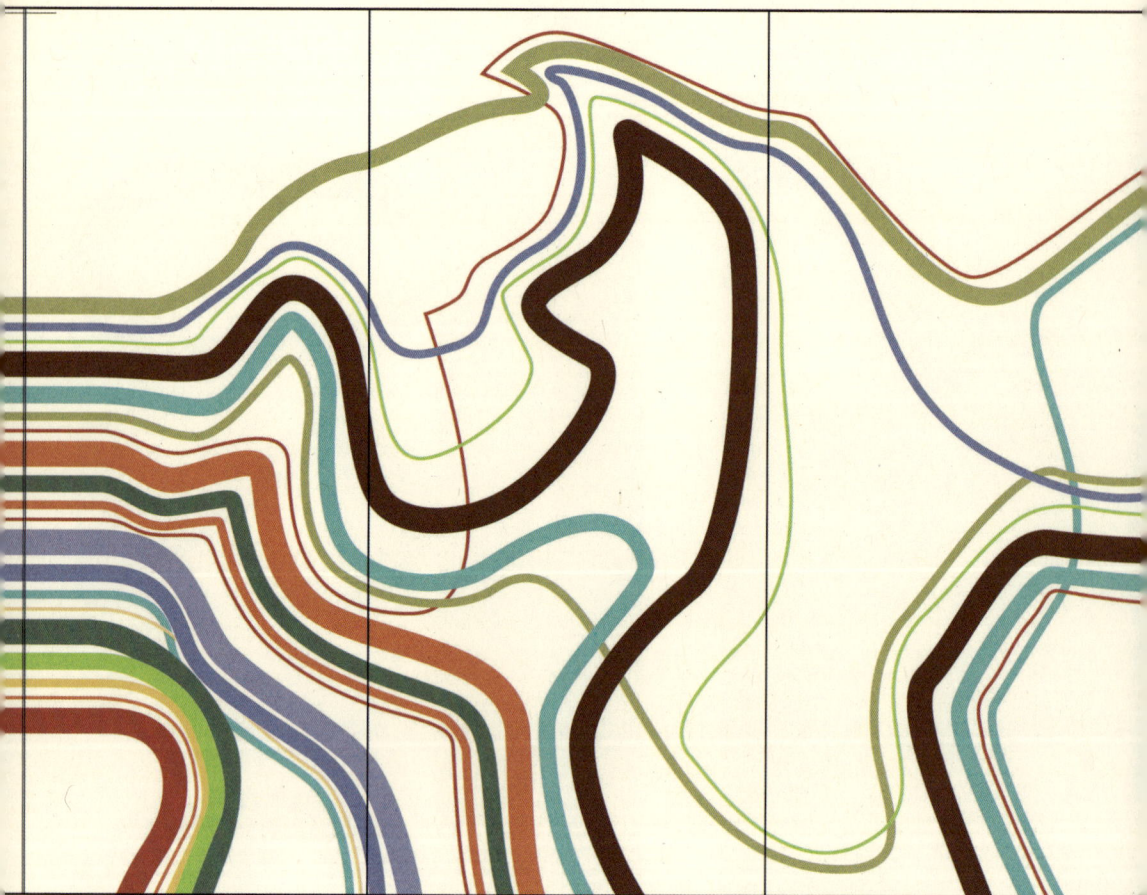

Experimentation with art and graphics was fundamental to the conceptual design development.

Project: Gambling Commission   Location: Birmingham

The concept for the cladding represents the building's DNA.

Project: Arup headquarters phases 2 and 3 ▬ Location: London

Project: Two bridges ▬ Location: Strabane, Northern Ireland

Remarkable objects. These two bridges are conceived as a series of stepping stones physically connecting cycle and pedestrian routes across Strabane. Composed from a series of stem-like forms, each module is a two-part component comprising a pre-cast concrete pier (or stem) with a lightweight steel deck (like a boat hull). One unit connects to another by means of two simple pin connections to form the bridge. A dramatic lighting scheme defines the sculptural quality of the bridges, creating a changing perspective to the river by day and night, ensuring the area is welcoming and safe to pedestrians.

10.2006

Projects in October ——— LDA ——— Great Newport Street ——— Glengall Bridge ——— University of Southampton

ELEVATION

LABS WEST ELEVATION

OFFICES EAST ELEVATION

SOUTH ELEVATION

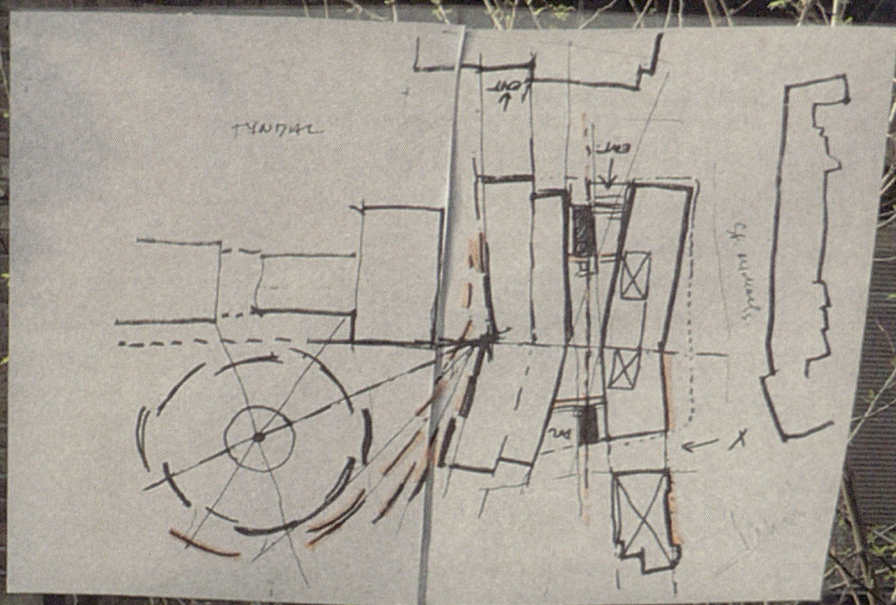

Amplifying the qualities of the London
Development Agency and its branding,
we have created a seamless journey
from the streetscape, to the workplace.
Light, colour, motif and form break down
the large rectilinear floor-plates and
express the agency's ambition for
London – a world class sustainable city.
We have brought the city into the building;
curved 'river walls', 'park-life' break-out
areas, planted hedges, and silhouettes
of the distinctive London skyline. The
concept is introduced at the organic pod,
where a dynamic internal 'wave wall'
leads visitors to a waiting area, while
an information zone linked by a ribbon
of deep pink, creates an interactive
space fronting the street. A combination
of 63kWh of photovoltaic panels and
21kWp of 14 wind turbines will provide
electricity for the office floors generating
3,397,000kWh of renewable energy and
reduce CO_2 emissions by 3,300 tonnes
during its lifetime. ━━━

Project: London Development Agency (LDA) ━━━ Location: Palestra, Southwark, London

Project: Great Newport Street ———— Location: London

Celebrating Soho's eclectic history, concept designs considered cladding this hotel in rubber, latex or PVC.

High density, high rise, high value public realm.

065

Project: Glengall Bridge — Location: Docklands, London

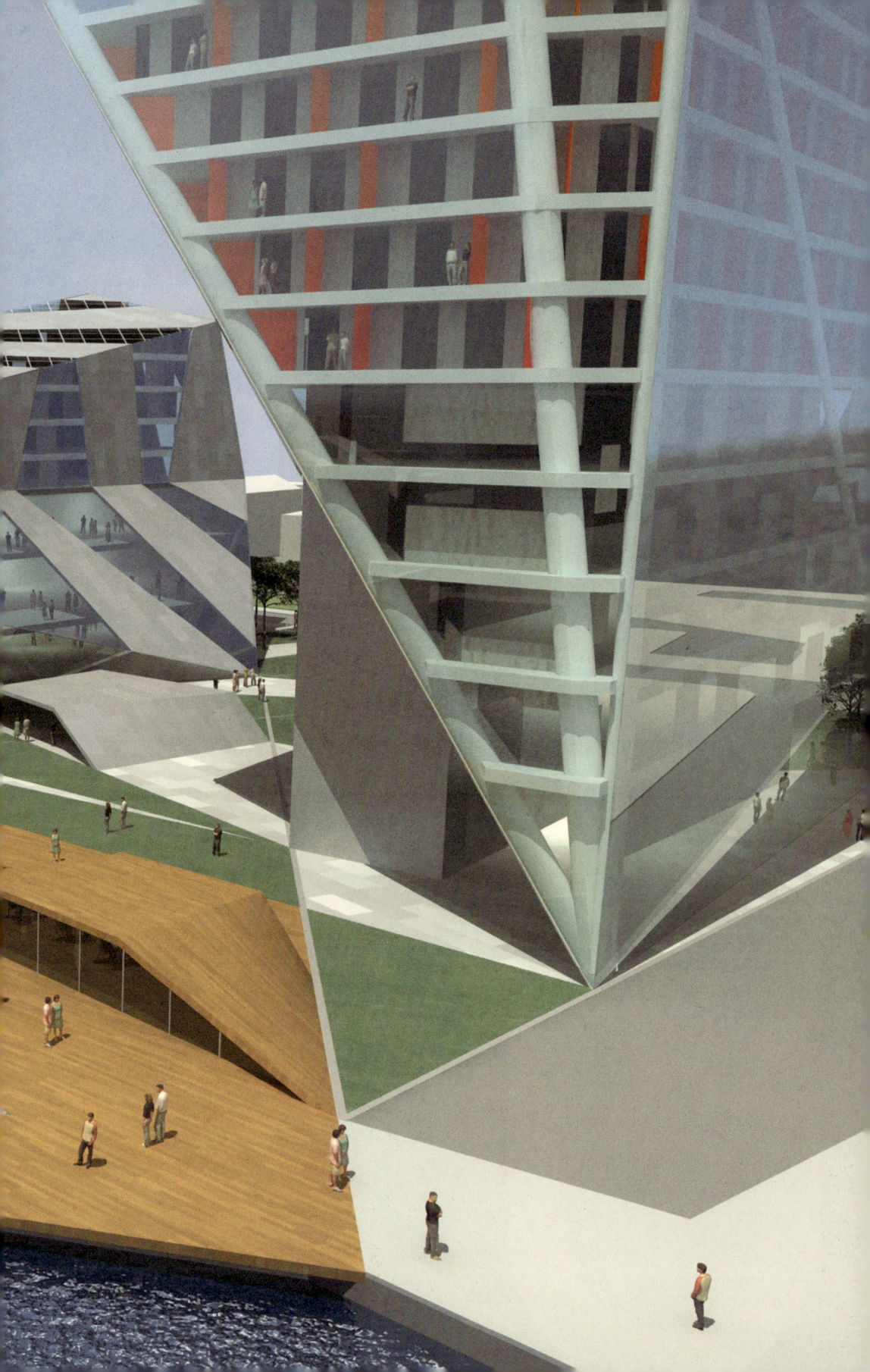

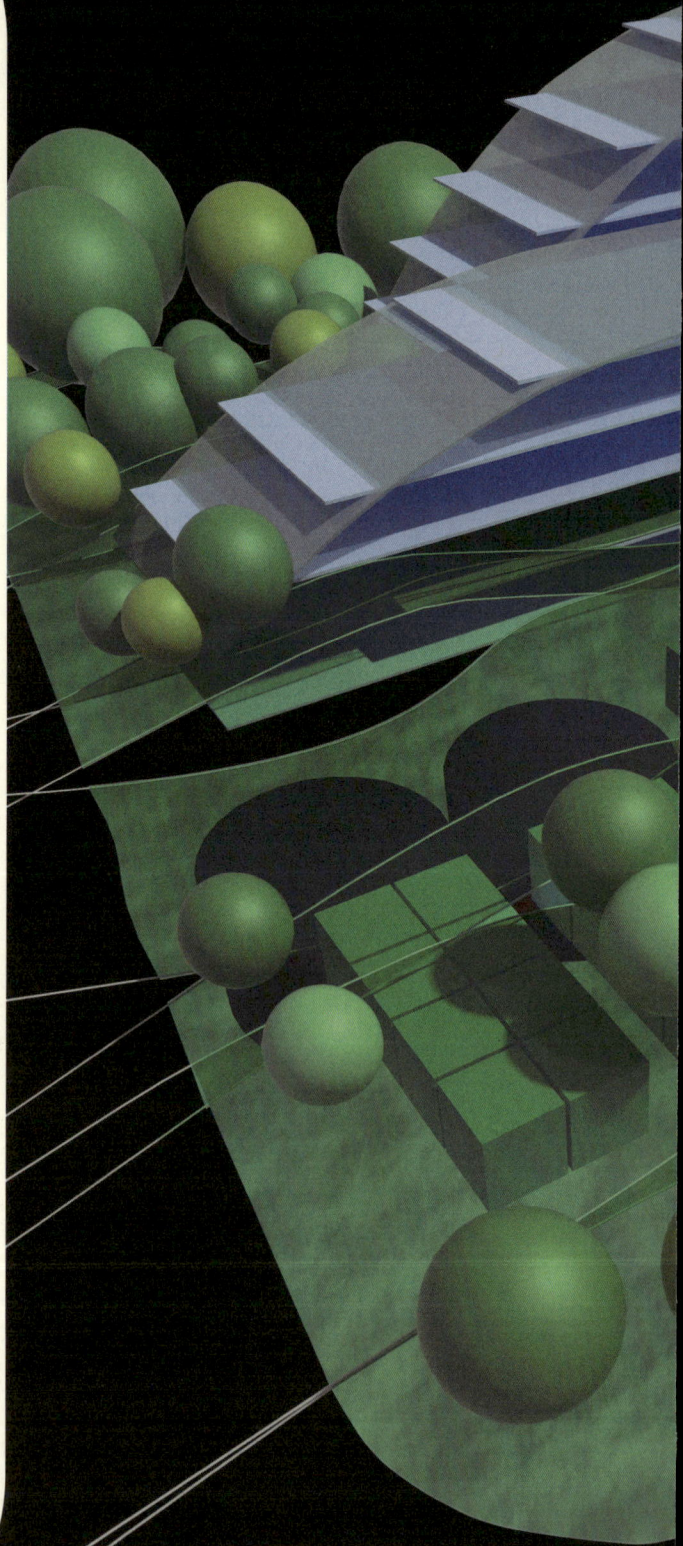

Project: Boldrewood Campus development ———— Location: University of Southampton

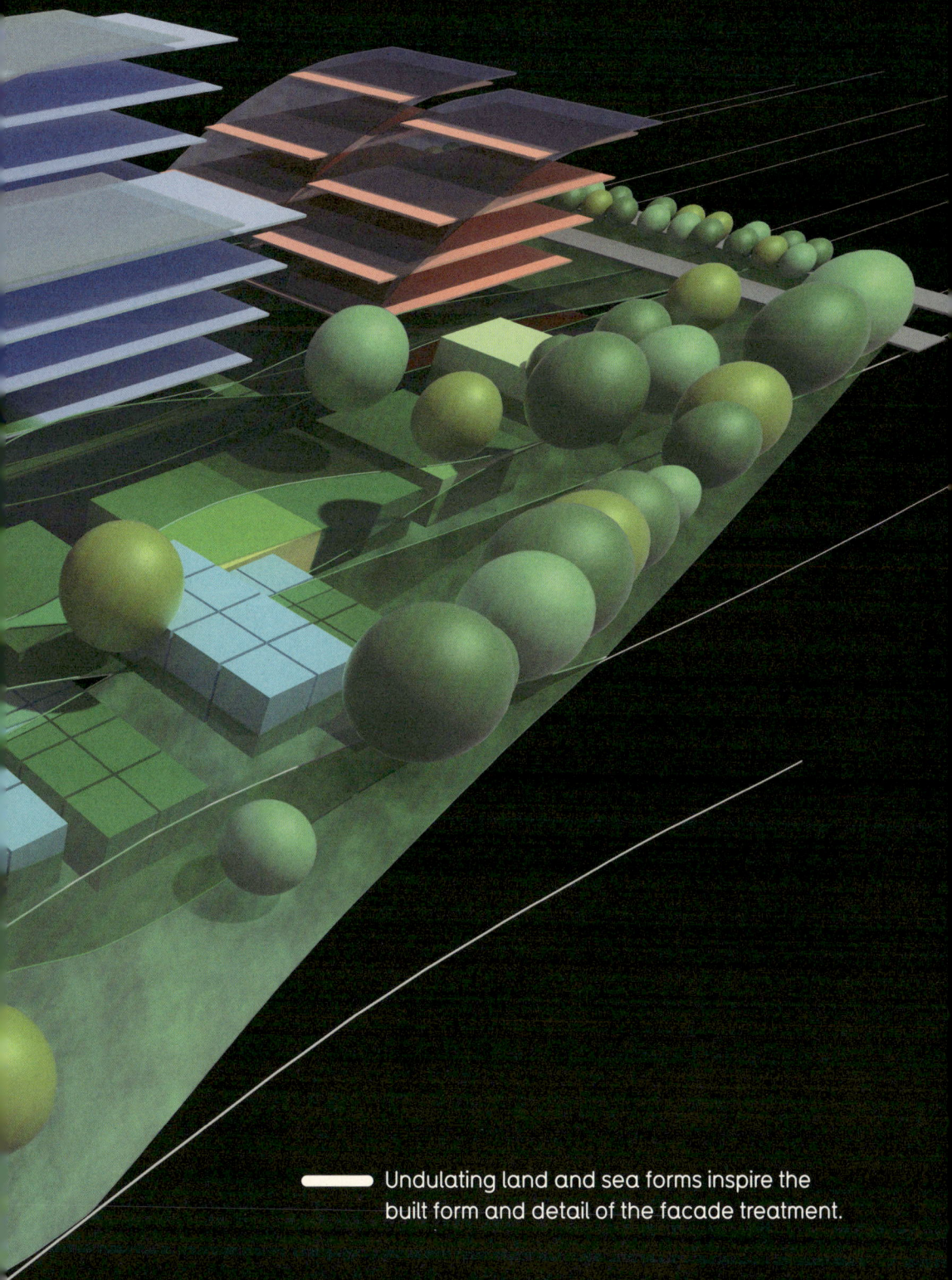

Undulating land and sea forms inspire the
built form and detail of the facade treatment.

11.2006

Projects in November ——— 399 Edgware ——— KICC ——— Tottenham Hale Bridge ——— St Mary-le-Port

How do you make high density human? We create space, identity and individual character. We create a landmark, but break down the scale, avoiding uniformity, and engaging with the surroundings. Create a mix of uses to make day-to-day living vibrant, and encourage a social infrastructure that can support a real sense of community (here we have incorporated a primary school with play areas on the roof). Then provide retail and leisure outlets which activate the street, but don't encroach on residents. Ultimately, give people environments that they can identify as their own. ▬▬▬

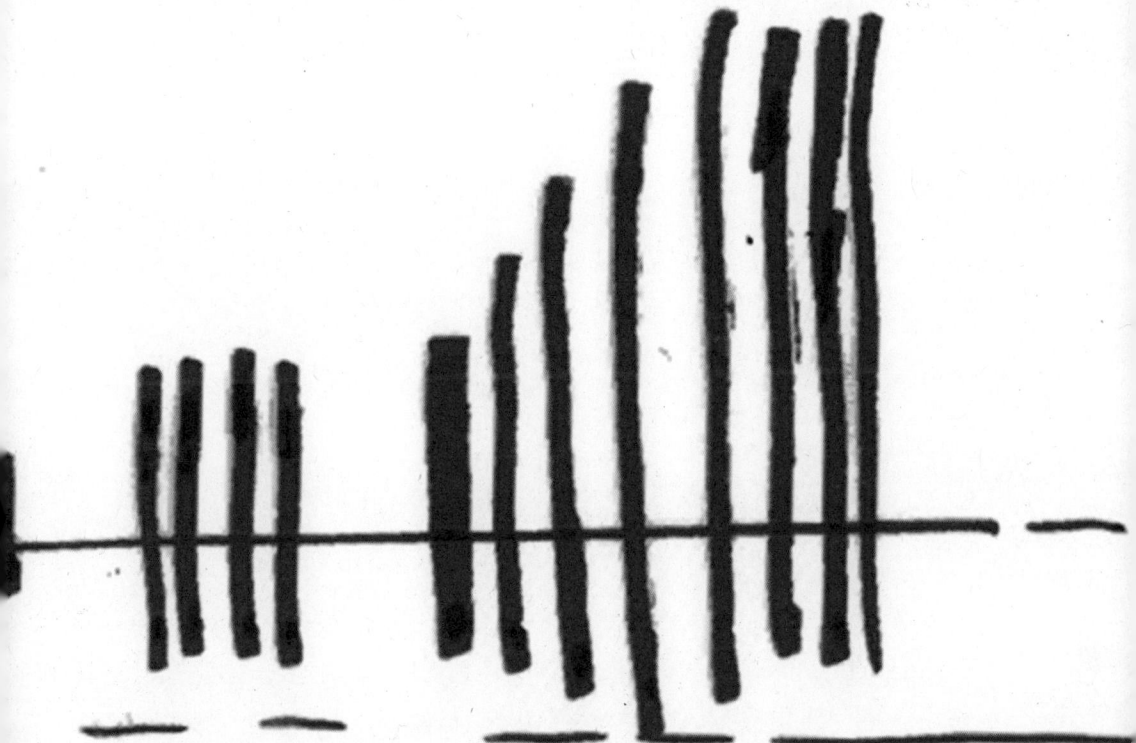

Project: KICC ▬▬▬ Location: London

A creation of spaces for congregating and celebrating.

080

Project: Pedestrian bridge ———— Location: Tottenham Hale, London

Your design concept
is very good, in fact
it's better than good,
it's world class...

Chairman of the judging panel.

The sinuous form responds to the changing path of the river on a site fronting Bristol's floating harbour.

12.206

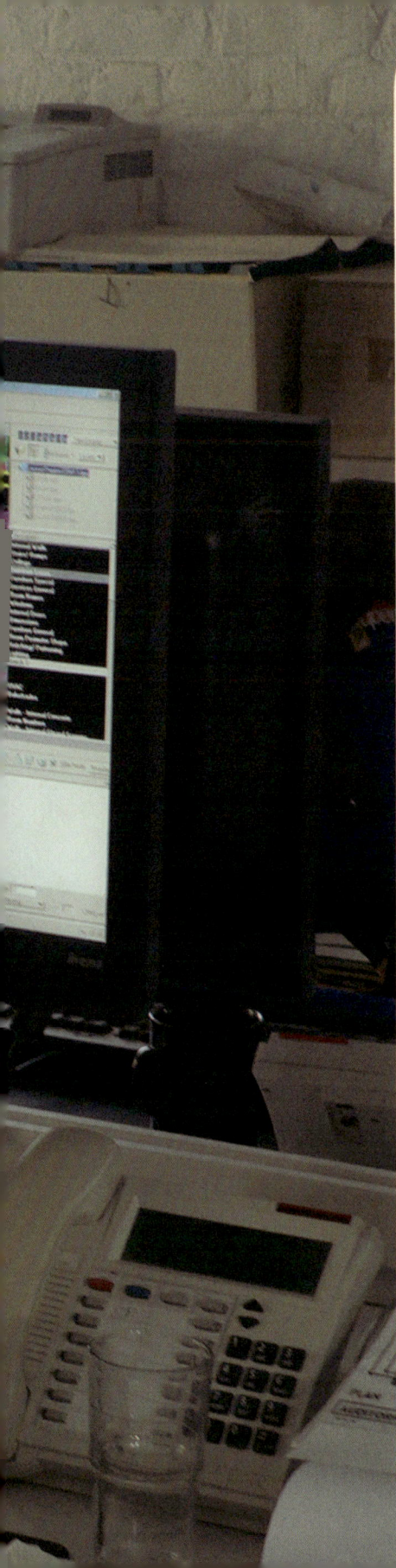

Projects in December —— Monument —— Lowther Castle and Gardens —— University of Liverpool

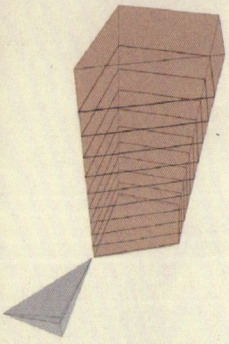

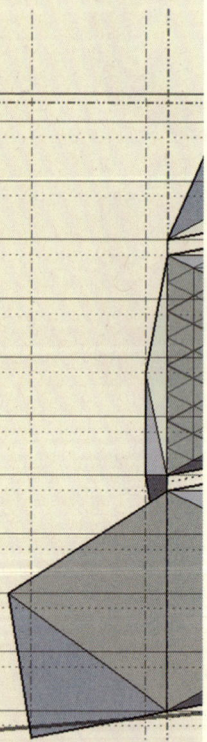

Project: Monument ———— Location: City of London

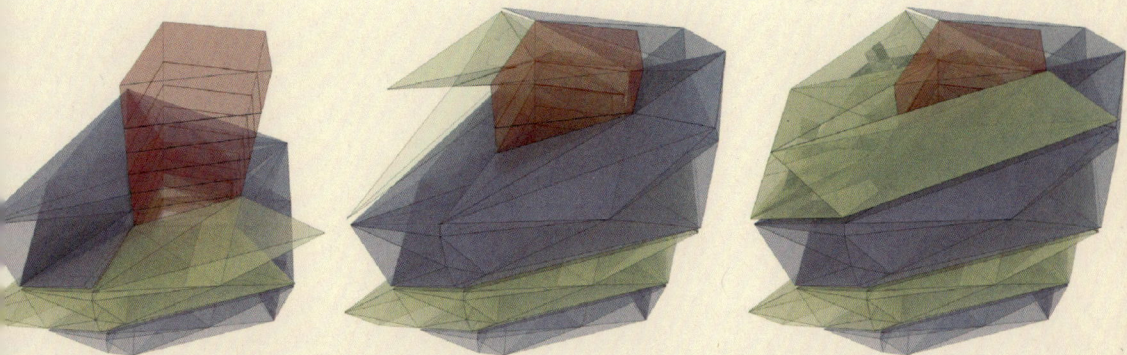

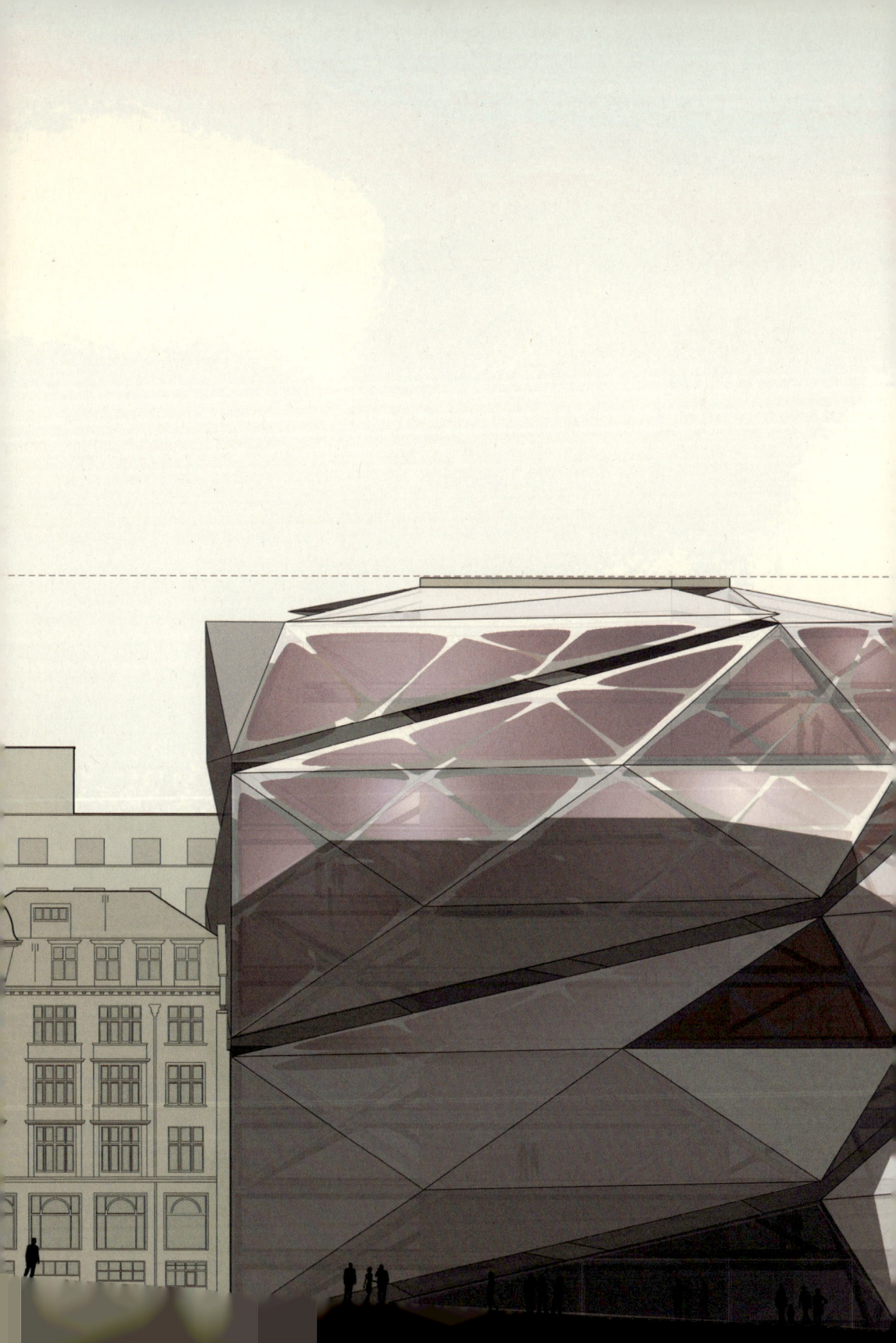

A sharp crystalline implant set in the very core of the City, playfully engaging with its historic context through the surprising reflections and environmental responsiveness of its spiralling, multi-faceted glass facade. An anti-monument of monumental impact.

Colin Fournier, Professor of Architecture and Urbanism, The Bartlett School of Architecture

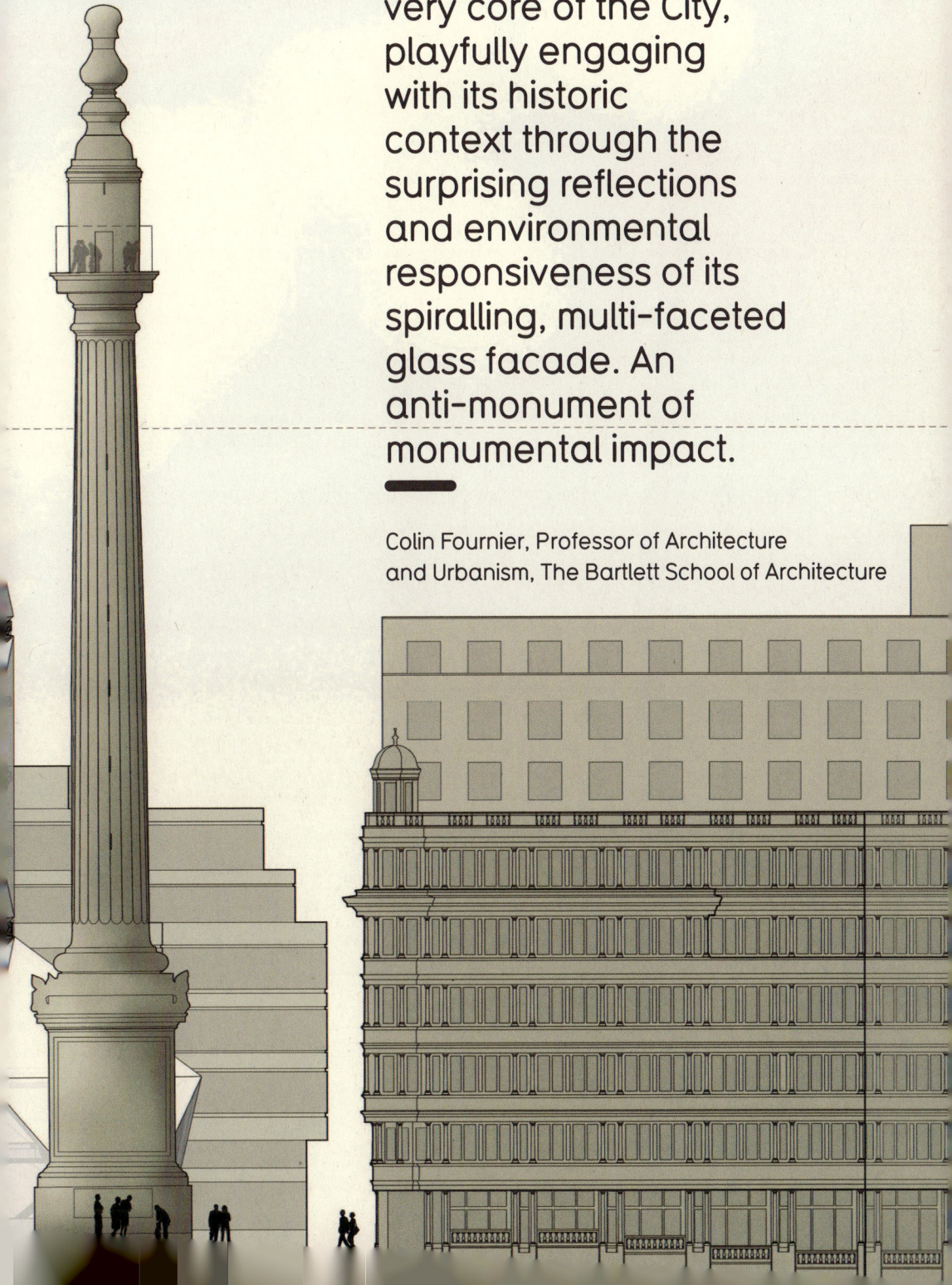

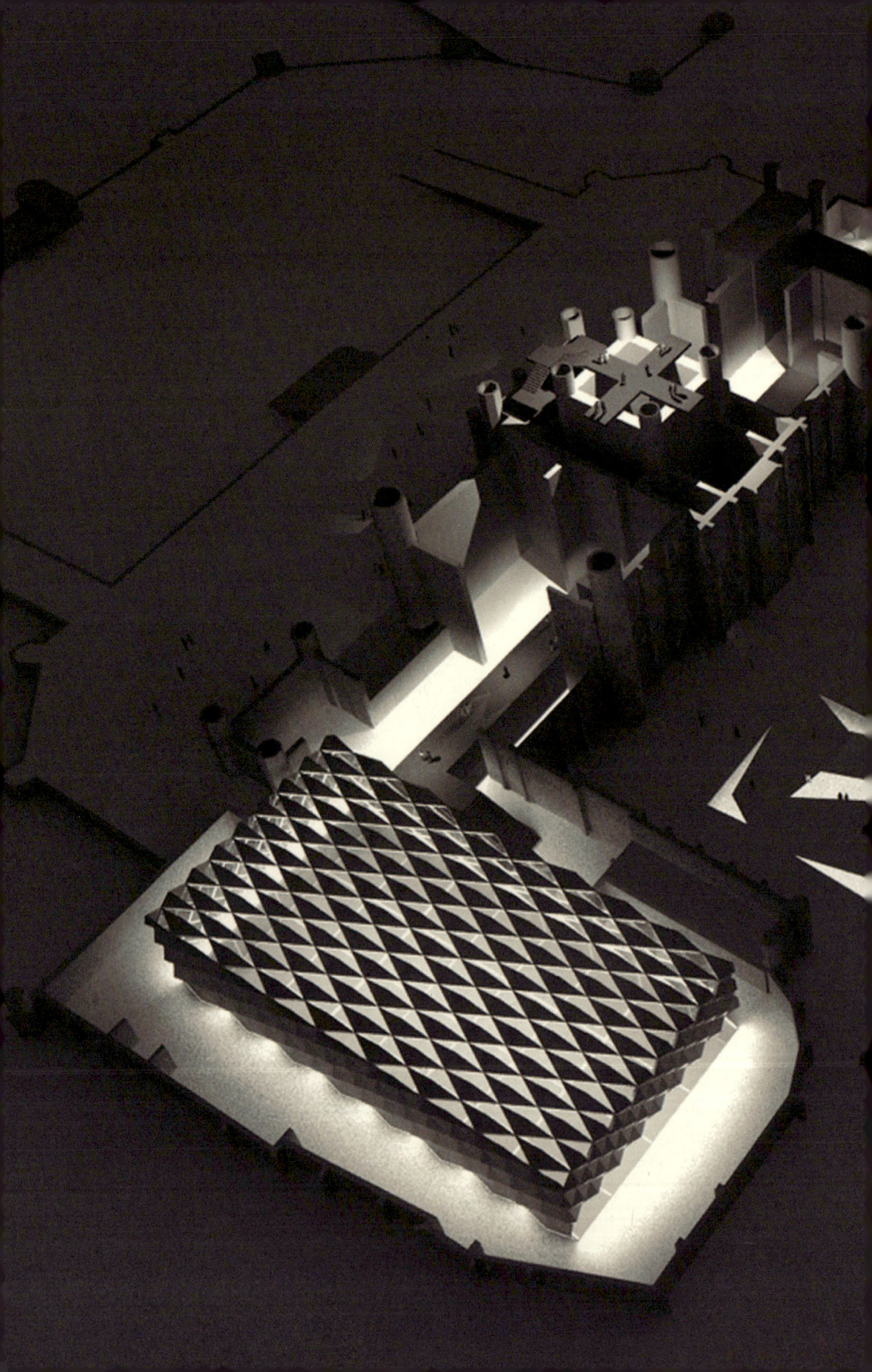

Project: Lowther Castle and Gardens ━ Location: Cumbria

A 19th century castle ruin and its gardens, of national significance, provides the setting for this unique project; a major new intervention of contemporary culture appealing to regional, national and international audiences. New architectural insertions are clear and modern, but complement rather than compete with the landscape, gardens and castle ruins. The major gallery below ground expresses its form only through its impact on the land above. The performance space, expressed as a series of large timber structures, resonates with the historic yew avenues of the surrounding park, and the amphitheatre opportunistically exploits the existing topography of the land. ▬▬▶

Project: Department of Engineering ━━ Location: University of Liverpool

An 'active learning lab' is housed in a 100 metre long structural truss.

01.2007

Projects in January —— Ashford Learning Campus —— SusCon

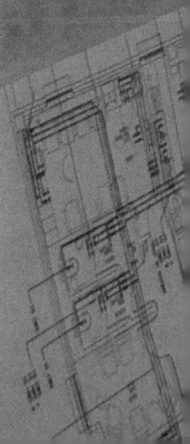

A246

At Ashford high speed Eurostar tracks run alongside the campus. This sense of travel, of movement, the aesthetics of transport, as well as Ashford's long history as a railway town, are interpreted in the interweaving, overlapping floor-plates of the building form. Each floor-plate 'moves' in plan around the cores and a central atrium, maintaining a constant width – as though they were a series of intersecting points giving a dynamic expression of the highly efficient series of spaces. Externally, linear zinc cladding evokes the romance of travel – the Japanese Bullet Train and the Greyhound buses of America. ━━━

Project: Ashford Learning Campus —— Location: Kent

Project: SusCon ━ Location: Kent

A new sustainable construction skills academy sits at the heart of Europe's largest regeneration project.

02 2007

Projects in February ———— University of Bristol ———— ITV ———— Dalston ———— Carabanchel 19

The concept of the Difference Engine and a clear vision from the mathematicians creates a circular form enhancing internal communications and views connecting the building to the city. The central space is a clear volume, a forum from which all users have both physical and visual connectivity and an interaction space where ideas are spread and world-class mathematics will be produced. ▬

Project: Mathematics Building ▬ Location: University of Bristol

Project: ITV — Location: Manchester

Looking at the bigger picture; stitching together transport and pedestrian connections addressing the wider regeneration of Dalston, and carving out an opportunity to fulfil the Mayor's 100 public spaces initiative.

Project: Dalston ———— Location: London

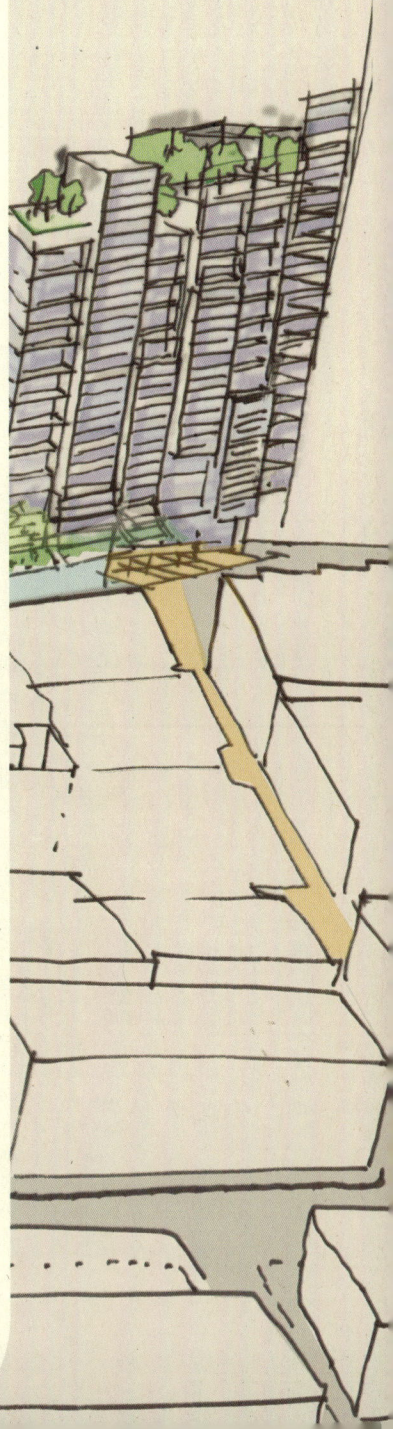

Environmentally effective and aesthetically powerful – adjectives usually reserved for private not social housing design. We have created Carabanchel 19 as part of the jigsaw of housing designed to create a city image for Madrid, providing legible living spaces which marry design with sustainable function. ▬▬ A louvered screen, a simple passive way of controlling solar gain, wraps and architecturally identifies the built form – a series of simple dual-aspect five and six storey blocks around three internal courtyards. Made of prefabricated units, the screening system is individually controlled providing shading and privacy to each apartment. As a result the facade of the building is ever-changing; a visual myriad to the surrounding streetscape, informing and challenging the occupiers to think about their immediate environment. ▬▬

We've had to go over
to Madrid to build a
significant sustainable
housing development.

Sheppard Robson, The Guardian, 19 February 2007

03.2.07

Projects in March —— Bessemer Building —— Aeronautics Faculty —— 40 Fountain Street

EVOLVE
BUSINESS 100%
90 g/m²
A4

EVOLVE
BUSINESS 100%
90 g/m² A3

EVOLVE
BUSINESS 100%
90 g/m²
A4

EVOLVE
BUSINESS

EVOLVE
BUSINESS

EVOLVE
BUSINESS

EVOLVE
BUSINESS 100%
90 g/m² A3

EVOLVE
BUSINESS

EVOLVE
BUSINESS

EVOLVE
BUSINESS

EVOLVE
OFF
80 g/m²

EVOLVE
OFF
80 g/m²

Project: Bessemer Building ——— Location: Imperial College, London

A structural facade defined by colour, sealed the conversion of this 60s building into laboratories.

The large scale wind scoop and turbines make the building an expression of its function.

Project: Aeronautics Faculty ━━━ Location: Exhibition Road, London

Project: 40 Fountain Street ━━━ Location: Manchester

04.207

Projects in April — InQbate — Northern General Hospital

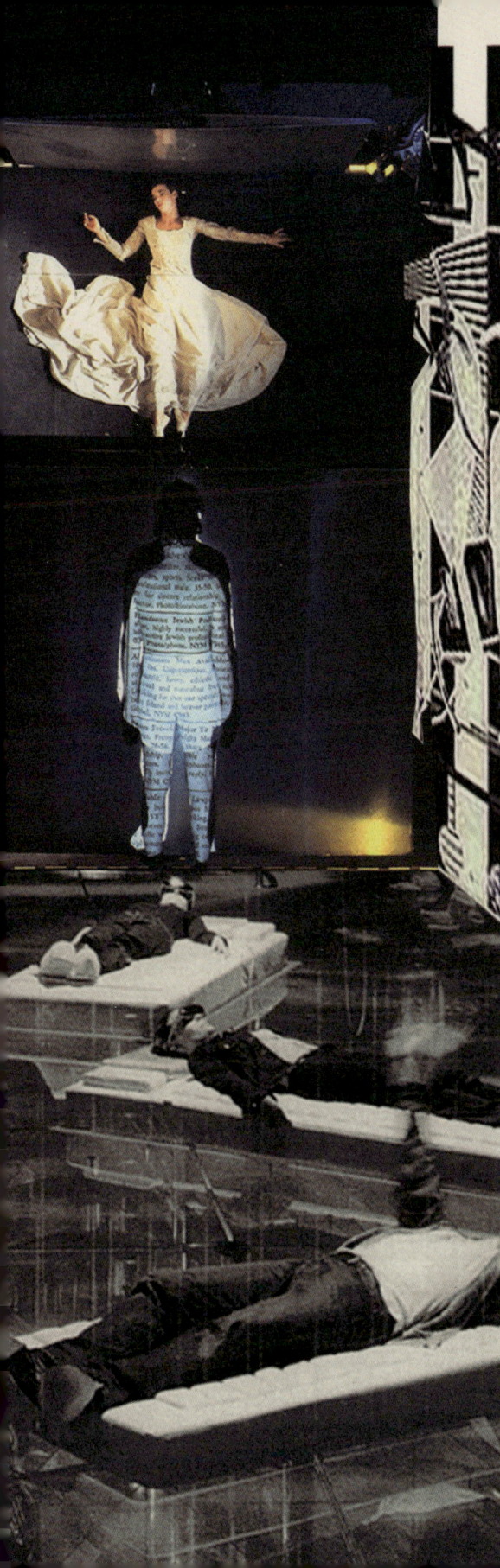

Project: InQbate, Centre of Excellence in Teaching & Learning in Creativity — Location: University of Sussex

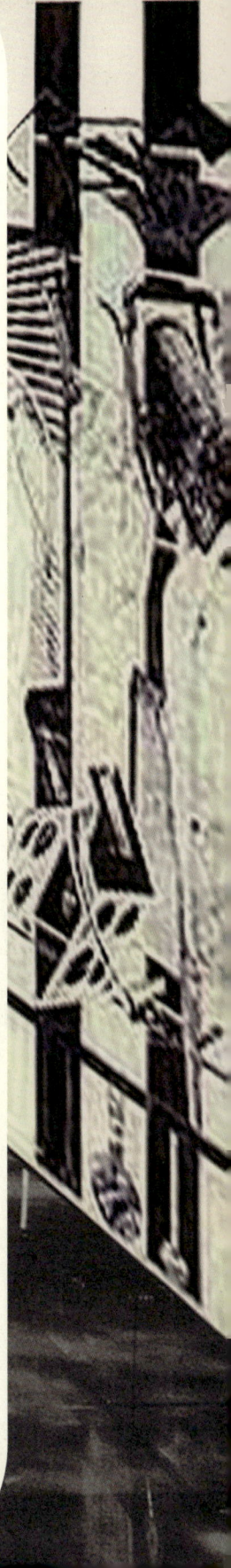

Conceived as a 100% wired and flexible 'white box' for creative learning.

Clarity of circulation and access to daylight assist with the creation of a healing environment.

Project: Northern General Hospital ━━━ Location: Sheffield

05.2007

Projects in May ——— Primrose Hill ——— Crawley New Town Hall ——— Lighthouse ——— Funlab

A sculptural form to create a unique address.

Project: Luxury residential development ———— Location: Primrose Hill, London

The concept is inspired by the civic meeting space and the public market hall. At the heart of the building these generate the form and image which is open, cool, informal and sustainable. This is further expressed in the responsive, dynamic fluctuating facade systems.

Project: New Town Hall ▬ Location: Crawley, Sussex

143

New standards? Surpass them; Lighthouse does. As a prototype it is the first housing design to achieve the Code for Sustainable Homes Level 6, the standard to which all new homes in the UK should be designed and constructed by 2016. ━━━ Don't stop there. Create a new model for future living and challenge the norm. Lighthouse does. It explores how housing can respond to changing demographics to create socially varied communities; encouraging lifestyles which are inherently 'light' on the world's resources. We have developed architectural solutions to modern living with sustainability integral to the design, creating houses that are attractive places to live in without compromising the occupant's quality of life. ━━━

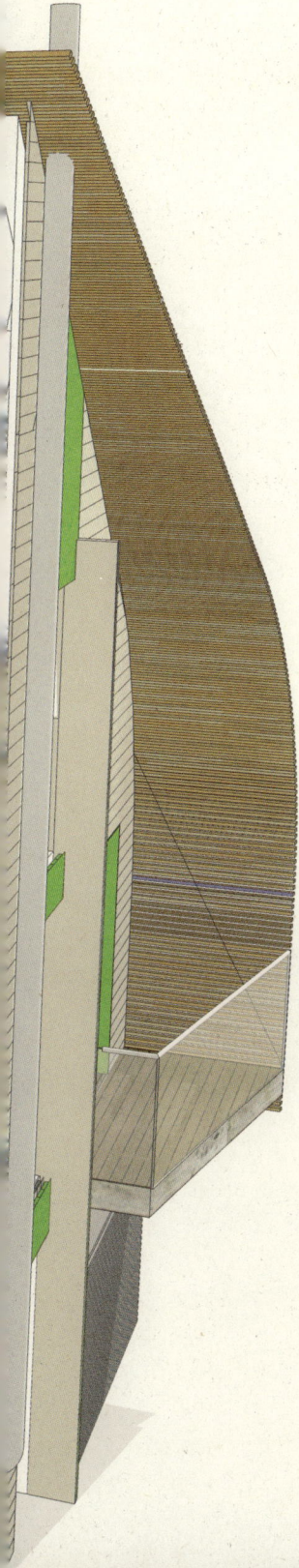

Project: Lighthouse ━━ Location: BRE, Watford

Project: Funlab   Location: London

LAUNCH WEBCAM POP-UP

VIEW ARCHIVE

A collaborative exhibition / comic - between collective welilkenicethings in the mycube in London and Jimmy Draht comics in Berlin - using specially designed online messaging software enabling particpants to see each other drawing in realtime and edit as they go along.

LAUNCH WEBCAM POP-UP

VIEW ARCHIVE

Sheppard Robson people

Jehane Abdelnour, Kate Ackermann, Nick Adams, Andres Aguilar, Jenna Al-Ali, Imran Ali, Vivienne Allen, Neal Allen-Burt, David Alleyne, Ethel Allison, Nigel Ames, Sebastian Appl, David Ardill, Quentin Armstrong-Barr, Ont Asvinvichit, Jaspal Atwal, Oezbir Aytekin, Sharon Baker, Darius Baniabassian, Gareth Banks, James Barker, Susana Barros-Costa, Gwen Barthelemy, Robin Base, Richard Bates, Antonietta Bavaro, Lee Bennett, Guy Bennett, Karen Bentley Smoker, Adolfo Berardozzi, Helen Berresford, Saurabh Bhandari, Tania Bhatia, Geeta Bhudia, Tony Billington, Mel Bissett, Marion Blender, Philip Bongomin, Liesl Botha, Rick Bowlby, Andrew Bowles, Daniel Brady, Craig Brailsford, Bruce Briggs, Andrew Brown, Linda Brown, Fionn Brown, Kathryn Brown, Claire Brown, Michael Bufalino, Helen Bunder-Smith, Dan Burr, David Burton, Robert Burwell, Ian Butler, David Callaghan, Dionne Callender, Michael Cambden, Sophie Campbell, Paula Carey, Victoria Casal, Aaron Casey, Nicholas Caulkett, Helen Chambers, Eric Chan, Raymond Chan, Daljit Chana, Luke Chandresinghe, Ronald Cheape, Ka Hung Cheng, Nini Cheng, Pierluigi Chinellato, Joanne Cho, James Church, Piotr Ciura, Breffni Clarke, Nadine Clarke, Sharon Clay, Steven Clews, Andrew Clifford, Paul Coates, Marilyn Coleman, Georgina Collins, Trevor Conley, Brian Connolly, David Connor, Lisa Cooper, Belarmino Cordero, Sean Corrigan, Jessica Cowie, Roger Crimlis, Hamish Crockett, Mary-Ann Crompton, Daniel Cruddace, Alejandro Cruz Amaya, Jo Curtis, Tony Cuss, Sam Danaipour, Jonathan Davies, Richard Davies, Daniella De Maria, Julia Dedman, Pia Degenhardt, Marcos Deus, Mark Dillon, Nikolaus Dohrn, Matt Dolman, Peta Drayton, Mary Durant, Liz Earwaker, Nittai Edelmann, Sarah Edwards, Ulf Eickelberg, Walter Eliskases, Chris Ellen, Martin Ellerby, Jaana Ellsasser, Gaui Erlendsson, David Eskdale, Jimi Estevez, Tim Evans, Tom Evans, Charlotte Evans, Rob Fairfield, Liesl Fireman, Graeme Fisher, Tim Fisher, Simon Flint, Lee Flowers, James Flynn, John Foat, Gregory Fonseca, Lara Ford, Bridget Ford, Kevin Forde, Martin Fox, Lucia Frondella, Tim Fry, Shu Man Fung, Suzanne Gaballa, Daniel Galleni, Renata Gatti, Robert Gauld, Andrew German, Guita Gharebaghi, David Giera, Rupert Goddard, James Grainger, Carlos Gravil, Mike Greatorex, Jack Gregory, Richard Griffin, Jonathan Griffiths, Justin Gurney, Jacqueline Haberer, Nicholas Hacking, Louisa Haines, Jacqui Hall, Mary Hamilton, Amy Hanley, Paul Harris, Leo Harris, Harriet Harriss, Mike Hart, Jonathan Hartnell, Ashley Harwood, Jafar Hasht-Rudi, Jo Hatwell, Claire Haywood, Eugene Healy, Pavla Heath, Catherine Hennessy, Anna Henshaw, Steven Hills, Harriett Hindmarsh, Eisuke Hiyama, Anna Hjartsjo, Angelia Hoffman Liard, Axel Hollfelder, Stuart Hood, Malcolm Hookings, Christian Horle, Alec Howson, Wanda Hu, Henry Humphreys, Carys Humphries, Tina Hurst, Janet Isaacs-Göttlieb, Sian Ives, Tori Jackson, Anna Jagiello-Hinde, Adam James, Emma James, Chris Jarvis, Simon Johns, Catherine Johnston, Lucy Jones, James Jones, Erica Jong, Andrea Jung, Katarzyna Jurkiewicz, Marion Juton, Krystina Kaczynski, Hiroki Kakizoe, Marcin Kaminski, Michael Kampkoetter, Lydia Kan, Anastasia Kapagerof, Stelios Kattou, Mark Keegan, Bob Keenan, Elizabeth Keenan, David Kelly, Barry Kendell, Angela Kennerknecht, Rekha Kerai, Dirk Kessler, Rob Kinder, Matthew King, Heike Kirsch, Jeff Kite, Kate Knuckey, Colin Ko, Roman Koester, Aud Koht, Agnes Koo, Mark Kowal, Tim Kreidel, Marianne Kudlich, Renza La Sala, Jerzy Lachowicz, Raymond Lam, Peter Lanyi, Jennifer Lau, Ian Laurence, Peter Lekberg, Daniel Leung, Marie Leyland, Frank Loehner, Paolo Longo, Anya Louw, Rodi MacArthur, Borja Marcaida, Dan Marcal, Mary Marr, Claudia Marx, Chris Mascall, Emma Masters, Laura Matthews, Lucy Matthews, Joseph Matthiessen, Martyn May, Simon McAllen, Rod McAllister, Malcolm McGowan, Danielle McIvor, Alastair McLauchlan, Simon McLean, Farah Md-Rahim, Peter Menken, Nabila Merniz, Louise Merrett, Adrienn Meszaros, Helen Millar, Dee Mistry, Emma Mitchell, Victoria Moffat, Killion Mokwete, Benjamin Molpeceres, Rachel Moody, Jennifer Moore, Christina Morgan, Rebecca Mortimore, Jens Moser, Ben Mott, Andy Moy, Christiane Mugele, Robert Myers, Nesha Naidoo, Jayvant Naran, Hanna Nasfeter, Virginia Newman, Patrick Ng, Mark Nicholson, Sara Nicholson, Catherine Nikolaou, Anastasia Nikopoulou, Paul Norbury, Milja Nykanen, Vivien O'Brien, Tony O'Brien, Stephanie O'Carroll, Seun Oduwole, Cara Oliver, Ann Olivier, Paul O'Neill, Anna O'Regan, Barbara O'Reilly, Sonia Pabla-Thomas, Kate Papageorgiou, Christina Pappa, Marco Parati, Jessica Parker, Matthew Parkes, Christelle Parmentier, John Parslow, Stuart Paterson, Emily Pavlatou, Dean Payton, Michael Peachey, Fleur Peck, Victoria Perkins, Nancy Peskett, Sophie Peters, Mark Petersen, Tim Pianta, Antonio Pisano, David Platt, Tim Polisano, Martin Pollock, Tony Poole, Christopher Poole, George Poppe, Sam Powell, Jackie Power, Howard Powsney, Neil Price, Lloyd Quansah, Reginald Quiling, Brooke Radtke, Fraser Rae, Michael Raithby, Joanna Rapp, Steven Rea, Ben Reed, James Reed, Markus Reisinger, Ed Reynolds, Erin Reynolds, Nick Ridout, Stephen Robins, Gavin Robinson, Claudio Romero, Felicity Roocke, Martin Rose, Mark Rostron, Sherralyn Rowlands, Ian Rudolph, Marius Ryrko, Renata Sa, Martin Sagar, Keith Sagar, Rajpal Sahota, Tamara Salamin, Pedro Santos, Bettina Sasse, Elizabeth Sawyer, Eugene Sayers, Johann Schnaus, Julian Schramek, Charles Scott, Nicholas Scott, Hassan Shaikh, Parag Sharma, Sam Sharpe, Andrew Shaw, Anna Shaw, Alan Shingler, Jacinta Siebert, Warwick Small, Justin Smith, Barry Smith, Alexander Smith, Christopher Smith, Joanne Smith-Lynch, Alex Solk, Stephen Solt, Lirong Soon, Nick Spall, Jason Speechly Dick, Anthony St Leger, Jonas Stahl, Jim Stannard, Tina Steel, Louise Strachan, Robert Studd, Neville Surti, Julia Sutcliffe, Tomek Swacha, Adrian Tanner, David Taylor, Fiona Tearle, Jeff Teerlinck, Anais Thomas, Mark Thompson, Nick Threlfall, Lee Ton, Kylie Tse, Takashi Tsurumaki, Stephen Tungay, Lee Turner, Julie Turner, John Tygier, Zoe Van Der Feltz, Karen Van Eeden, Nicola Van Waegeningh, Saritha Varikkara, Simeon Viveash, Jo Walker, Laimin Wan, Tamsin Ward, Jayne Washbourne; Tim Webster, Barbara Weightman, Yaochun Wen, Douglas Wheatland, Daniel White, Helen Wildgust, John Williamson, Dominic Wilson, Suzanne Wilson, Daniel Winder, Suzi Winstanley, Hannah Wong, Nicholas Wood, Jamie Wood, Chris Woodhouse, Kathy Woodward, Andrea Wright, Felix Wu, Anuschka Wyatt, Brent Yttrup, Zetty Wan Zakaria, Consultants: Graham Anthony; Graham Francis; Anthony Furlong; Paul Watkins.